When to Keep Your Mouth Shut

Say it Best, by Saying Nothing at all

By

Benjamin Kennet

GW00480526

When to Keep Your Mouth Shut

Copyright © 2017

ISBN: 9781520427003

Warning and Disclaimer

Publisher Contact

Skinny Bottle Publishing

books@skinnybottle.com

Shut up!

That is probably one of the most overused phrases that people hear so often. It can be an expression or an aggressive statement that imposes on someone to just shut it. Sometimes, it becomes a heated argument that originally started from what seems to be a great casual conversation over coffee. However, how the conversation was steered during the exchange of ideas between the speaker and listener will determine if this will end up well or not.

On average, we speak about eight thousand words per day. How these words are expressed will depend on a number of external factors, such as emotion, preoccupation, and many more. In a world where everything is like a mini-competition, we want to express ourselves and voice out our opinions. However, this intention can be something positive for one who is airing out his or her insights, but it can be negatively absorbed by the one who hears it.

So why do we have to know when to shut up, and why is this such an important thing to do? This is because communication is vital to our existence, but we tend to either underuse or abuse it. We are not properly utilizing the wonderful art of communication. We just speak, and sometimes, we speak first then think later.

Learning the delicate balance of shutting up or speaking up is considered as a difficult skill to master, or even to understand. Even the most experienced conversationalists still struggle with it. You can be too "by the book" in terms of the mechanics of proper understanding, but this practice can easily be disrupted by mood, and then boom! Conflict arises.

The succeeding chapters will cover the basics of why we talk a lot, what should be done about it, and how we can decrease the chances of reaching a boiling point that will cause emotional bursts. But in a nutshell, when you are in doubt, it would be better to opt to keep your mouth shut rather than risk speaking your mind and potentially offending someone else. When you don't say anything, you will never be placed into hot water. However, the delicate balance hangs because there will also be times that you have to speak up. This is why it is important to know when to do it and how to do it right.

The Science of Why We Talk Too Much

There is a good chance that you are talking too much yet you don't notice it, and in fact, science confirms it. Humans are social and emotional by nature, and it is deep rooted in our DNA to use our senses as an instrument to help us thrive and survive. Communication is a vital part of our existence, regardless of whether you are the most introverted person in class or the most extroverted employee in the office. However, this is the part where the problem starts.

Research confirms that when we talk to our friends, colleagues, or someone we just met, up to sixty percent of the things we speak about focus on ourselves. The rate is even higher when it comes to online chatting and social media, where it reaches up to eighty percent. It is understandable that we take pride of how we carry ourselves, our achievements, and our passions. Unfortunately, the way in which our words are perceived is not always the same, and there is a good chance that the words we speak would be misconstrued. In fact, even established psychologists from Harvard observed that there are individuals who are willing to shell out some cash just to gain the opportunity to share facts about themselves.

Communication is part of our daily lives. It allows us to express ourselves and let our opinions be heard. That should've been such a peaceful exchange of ideas, but because we see things differently, conflicts and misunderstandings may arise. Talking about ourselves makes us feel better. It boosts our confidence and generally improves our mood. There is nothing wrong about it, that is until we go overboard in terms of talking too much or we meet an inappropriate audience. As we go along with our daily activities, we will surely encounter individuals with varying attention spans, and that actually includes you. Attention spans can be significantly lengthy, or unfortunately brief, and when we say brief, that's as little as five to eight seconds.

Ideally, a conversation should be an exchange of ideas – an absolute give and take and sharing an equal opportunity. That being said, it means that half the time, you should be listening attentively. No one should be in control because the opportunity is equal for both parties. This may sound easy, but it is rarely utilized because a typical conversation usually has a speaker and a listener, and often both parties should take turns being the speaker and a listener. Staying quiet and listening are two very powerful tools in academics and business, but not everyone can use them properly.

According to Peter Bregman:

Silence is a greatly underestimated source of power. In silence, we can hear not only what is being said, but also what is not being said. In silence, it can be easier to reach the truth.

Mark Goulston, a known business psychiatrist, states that the importance of listening and paying attention during the stages of conversation lies in the following aspects:

Business Stage: This is where everything builds up – tension, precision, interest, everything. Every time a conversation is initiated, an impression is also created, and if the impression is not that good, there is an elevated chance that the conversation may cause indifference or friction.

Feel-Good Stage: This is the stage of great experiences and the release of tension. Agitation is minimized in this stage, and this is when the focus is on you and what it is that you have to say. However, when you are focused on yourself, you may fail to observe whether the other person is still listening or not.

Recovery Stage: This is a stage in which you experience a common urge to speak more in an attempt to recapture the listener's interest because you want to regain the attention that might have been lost during the previous stage.

As you can see, a conversation is a delicate balance of exchange. Even if you think you are good at starting conversations, this does not guarantee that you're good at concluding them. Every conversation is like a "walking on eggshells" experience. It is very important that the essence of "give and take" is utilized all the time.

According to coach and radio show host Marty Nemko, you can use the traffic light method to somehow restrain the chatter. The method goes like this:

A green light is open within the first twenty seconds. This is the time when the listener pays attention and likes what you're saying. The next one, which is the yellow light, is the next twenty seconds, which comes with an increased risk that the listener is losing his or her interest that may be caused by long-winded or self-centered words coming from you. Now, as you reach the forty-second mark, this duration becomes the red light. This means that you have to stop or you might be in danger of annoying your listener, which may end anywhere from a discontinued conversation to a potentially abrasive conclusion.

Going back to Goulston's points, you might need to determine why you talk so much. Why we talk can stem from a wide variety of reasons. This can be due to confidence issues, especially when you are trying not just to capture the attention of your listeners, but to impress them as well. This is extremely evident in job interviews because you're trying to weave impressive opinions, because of which you may end up formulating repetitive statements. Some utilize talking as an outlet for stress, where they find a sense of release from frustrations and internal conflicts. There are some people who are excessive talkers because this might be the environment in which they grow up, or this is the nature to which they adapted. Unfortunately, speaking too much too often can be destructive without us even noticing it.

Can you resist the pressure to speak?

This is such a challenging and thought-provoking question that we sometimes ignore. Speaking is very hard to resist, especially if you have an opinion that you want others to hear. Speaking is hard, but you know what is harder? Listening.

One of the most common sayings states that the problem with today's society is that we listen not to understand – we listen to reply. Instead of understanding what the other person says, you are formulating your next reply inside your head. This makes communication very hard for most people because aside from these factors, there are also other variables, such as emotions and perception, which directly affect the process.

In an academic or professional setting, you usually lose the conversational battle if you have to answer your own question. If you allow a harmonious exchange with your classmates or peers, you will be surprised that there are changes that you will observe that were not there during the time that you were busy building yourself up during conversations.

Understanding Your Emotional Limits

We have already identified ourselves as emotional by nature. However, the emotional limits still vary from one person to another. Some can cry at the drop of the hat, while others need some warming up. Some individuals are quite explosive, whereas others overly sensitive.

Our emotional limits are those invisible boundaries that divide our feelings from others. Not only do these boundaries mark off where your feelings begin and end, it also helps you shield your feelings during the times that you feel vulnerable and to allow others to access your feelings whenever you feel safe and intimate. An individual is considered to have healthy emotional limits when he or she respects and understands his or her own feelings and thoughts, such that he or she has a concrete definition of self-respect and embraces his or her own uniqueness. The words "Yes" and "No" are two very powerful words that can define emotional limits. The former allows acceptance and permission, whereas the latter strengthens the existing emotional boundaries. Emotional limits promote order in life. They allow an individual to feel secure in his or her own skin. It also encourages intimacy.

There is a difference between a limit and a compromise. A limit can be something that you may not know until it is tested, while a compromise is a process where you consciously promote give and take. On the other hand, enmeshment is a process of neglecting who you are as a person or disregarding what your needs are just to please another person. Sacrificing a portion of yourself just to please another may work, but it can only be a band-aid solution. Later, you will realize that you may have gained a person's attention or became engaged in a relationship, but at the painful expense of losing yourself in the process.

What is the connection between communication and emotional limits? Given that there is no such thing as an emotionless conversation, as emotion is integral to our existence, it is very important to know your limits, even relative to the simplest conversations that you will ever encounter. Once you have found yourself, including your strengths and weakness, you gain control on a more positive and worthwhile note.

On the other hand, being such an overly emotional person can hurt you, your career, and even the ones you love. Your actions, both verbal and non-verbal, can be misconstrued. Just like when Beast started to woo Belle in Beauty and the Beast, everyone told him that he must control his temper. I believe it is the best time to take over and understand your emotional limits further.

When to Shut Up

Now we go to the main game. Every single day, there will always be an opportunity to shut up. We all see different characters in media who speak the blunt truth. It is normal that we love those who speak the truth, especially when that truth is not about us. Because of varying plots or personalities that are shown on TV, we always receive mixed signals on who or what is right.

Mixed Signals

We have found these two quotations that you might have encountered in the past – one is old, and the other is way older:

It is better to keep your mouth closed and let people think you are a fool than to open it and remove all doubt. — Mark Twain

A person who asks a question is a fool for five minutes; a person who doesn't is a fool forever. — Chinese proverb

Mark Twain encourages us upfront to just shut up. On the other hand, the proverb motivates you to speak your mind. The truth is, if there is confusion, it is best to shut up. Speaking up may hurt someone's emotions or opinions, and this action can end up into even more confusion, especially if you are giving an opinion that contradicts what others may have said.

Challenging Scenarios

There are a lot of opportunities that appear in front of you on a daily basis. Such scenarios often lead to conversations that induce verbal friction and can be confrontational at times. Some of these situations include the following:

- You have to meet someone who showed up half an hour late, which lead to a domino effect of you being late to the next appointments.

- Someone in the compound has been allowing his dog to scatter the trash. You saw this person walking his dog again.

- Your colleague talks really loud on the phone next to your desk.

- You are a manager and you are disappointed with the performance of your subordinate, or, you are a subordinate and you are disappointed with the performance of your boss.

- Your boyfriend loves whole wheat bread, but this is not really your thing.

- A colleague has been coughing for several days already, and it has started to irritate you.

- You saw a customer yelling at the barista.

- A young man cut the line in front of an elderly woman.

These scenarios give you an option to speak up or shut up. But how can you really know if the response that you give can be considered the best in every situation?

Speaking Up: The Benefits

When a person does not speak up, it often leads to passive-aggressive behavior. This is a reaction in which you rebel through obstructionist, subversive actions aimed at damaging the person you are having friction with.

As you can see in the list we have previously mentioned, there is a situation in which your colleague is talking so loud over the phone that it starts to get on your nerves. If you are the type of individual who is considered as passive–aggressive and who opted to shut up and not speak up, this colleague of yours will be experiencing cold professionalism within the next couple of days. You will subconsciously make more noise, such as banging folders or opening a bag of chips and making sure that it is heard. You will find yourself antagonizing the other colleague. Initially, the passive–aggressive person may think that he or she chose not to be the rude colleague because of opting to suffer in silence. However, the so-called obstructionist resistance can actually be the worse set of actions when compared to confrontation. Sometimes, we neglect the non-verbal actions that we subconsciously do.

Actions speak louder than words. There is no better example to which we can relate this type of behavioral intervention. We just need to find the perfect approach to deal with the problem without dealing too much emotional damage.

Shutting Up: The Benefits

Although speaking up prevents the development of such passive–aggressive responses, there are still times that it is better to just shut up. This is especially important when you are placed in a highly emotional state that could cloud your ability to think and speak clearly. This can be a fight or flight situation for you, and sometimes, when we give in to our emotions and speak our mind, the results are usually not good. Whether the emotions are positive, such as overexcitement or just plain bliss, or on the negative side, such as extreme anger or dismay, it would be best to let your emotions simmer down and allow yourself to think clearly.

In one of the listed situations, you have a neighbor whose dog always makes a mess. Airing out your concerns can lead to confrontations that could have been prevented in the first place. Because the neighbor can be unaware of his dog's actions, this issue can be considered by your neighbor as not a problem at all. This is a fact that we have to deal with on a daily basis – people around us can be insensitive to what is happening around them. Conflict occurs when you confront the neighbor and he retaliates verbally, or worse, physically. Confrontation can be interpreted as a hostile and unjust reaction.

In these types of situations, you are leaning towards speaking a lot more than what you intended. This is because of a clouded judgment, which is reflected not just in how you deliver your words, but also in what words are actually coming out of your mouth. Your word choices become stronger and more abrasive. Combine this with a strong tone of delivery and you got a very powerful weapon that is emotionally destructive, not only to the person you're talking to but also to yourself. Moreover, when you speak more words pertaining to the problem, there is a good chance that your other concerns, which have been previously suppressed, will be brought up. Originally, the concern revolves around the mess that the dog makes, but the confrontation will also cover how loud your neighbor plays his music or how the cigarette butts he throws around irritates you, and the list could go on.

Then later, you'll regret saying those words because your nerves already calmed down. You see, we all have our own battles every single day, but we have full control of how we react to the situations thrown at us. We only have two very tricky options: speak up or shut up.

The problem in the workplace is that we tend to share our opinions and provide unsolicited advice. Opinions are personal takes, which can be the "right" opinion from the speaker's point of view, in the same way that it can be the "wrong" choice from the listener's perspective. This is why it is important to think very well before voicing out an opinion, a grievance, or even advice because sometimes, it is more beneficial to keep our opinions to ourselves. This is evident in individuals who are very vocal about their opinions and emotions. These people, despite airing these opinions out with sincere intentions because it is part of their norm, are often misunderstood.

Setting Your Own Rules

There is no definite rule imposed on whether or not it is time to speak up or shut up. It is a matter of timing and sound decision. In general, the most common mistake that we can do is going overboard, that is, talking too much or failing to communicate. Of course, anything done in excess will not lead to something fruitful or positive. Know your battles, and make sure you know them well. The best way to formulate your own rules is to understand yourself more first. This should be the foundation of your ability to communicate with others. Once you have acquainted yourself with your fears, limits, morals, and values, you become more equipped to deal with every possible situation you will encounter. Some individuals have several rules that they impose on themselves, such as the 10-second rule (or 15-second rule for others). The 10-second rule is applied when you are in a state of heightened emotion and you want to speak up. By counting ten seconds, the elevation of your emotion will subside, and your mind clears up, thereby allowing a more calm expression of what you want to say. This is very effective in times that you are very angry or very happy, and due to the sudden emotional surge, you are prone to speaking a lot more, which may lead to a negative conclusion. If your emotions have simmered down before you open your mouth, you can be sure that the results are more acceptable and would promote a more harmonious verbal exchange.

Bear in mind that shutting up most of the time, or remaining quiet all the time, is considered as a very dangerous attitude. It allows the buildup of stress, which can eventually show up as different manifestations. A large percentage of illnesses and other health conditions we have today are caused by stress. That is why it is important to select when to shut up, and not shut up all the time. When you keep quiet, it can be a better choice sometimes, but this is only a temporary solution.

Ways to Divert Emotional Spillover

It has been scientifically proven that we subject ourselves to varying levels of stress from the moment we wake up to the time we hit the sack. This is on top of the stress that we create for ourselves based on the choices that we make. Our emotional gauge ramps up, and before we know it, we experience tremendous waves of agitation and in the end, we burn out.

While there are a lot of situations that lead us to the choice of speaking up or shutting up, there are also a lot of choices we can do to somehow divert or create a channel to release such emotional spillovers. You can have something that can be done briefly, like short walks around the park or breathing exercises to release some tension. You can also allocate an entire day or two for this process, such as a short staycation or a day at the beach. You have a lot of choices on how to reduce the stress buildup and to allow yourself to address the situations you have to deal with on a daily basis. These options will never solve the root cause, but they can significantly take away a chunk of burden and allow you to take a breather.

Doctors strongly recommend physical activities as an effective stress-buster. Simple activities, such as stretching, walking, cycling, or even small-level gardening, can help relieve stress. You can listen to music, take long showers, or tend your pet fish – the possibilities are actually endless.

Walking

Walk it off, period. This is considered as the most effective stress reducer that you can use without even noticing. When you walk around, you allow yourself to be distracted by the things around you. Numerous studies have confirmed that walking offers significant stress reduction after several minutes. Not only does it provide tension release, it also stimulates the increased production of endorphins. It is like getting the benefits of eating chocolate to improve mood without the added calories. Walking also improves blood circulation and stamina, which can help in the oxygenation of the brain. This promotes clarity of the mind and stability of your mood.

Stretching

Stretching allows to you feel more relaxed and at ease. Stretching can be done anywhere and anytime, and the tension leaves your neck, back, and other muscles, which promotes comfort.

Accomplish Small Daily Projects

You can channel your attention toward accomplishing small tasks on a daily basis. These activities can be something that can be completed after several minutes or hours, thus offering a great sense of accomplishment compared to the amount of effort you've poured in to complete it. These projects may include arranging books, sorting photos, overhauling the wardrobe, or others like reading books, starting a blog, or repurposing old stuff.

Rekindle an Old Hobby

At the back of our heads, we always wanted to be distracted in a positive way. One of the most worthwhile kinds of distraction is to rekindle a hobby or passion that will allow you to divert your attention into something you love doing. Crocheting, painting, and writing are some of the things you can do to keep your senses refreshed and less agitated. What's more, it yields progress and accomplishment at the same time. Who knows, it can even grow into something fantastic.

Smell the Flowers

This is literally one of the little things that we tend to miss due to our busy and preoccupied routines. In relevance to gardening, allow yourself to appreciate nature and the positive vibe it brings. Smell the flowers and herbs from time to time, or listen to the chirping birds that keep you entertained every morning. Aside from the decision on whether to speak up or shut up, it will also completely depend on our choices if we will pour our attention towards the good side of life. When we concentrate our minds on the good things, better happenings will follow.

Gardening

If you want to channel your green thumb into something worthwhile, try small-scale gardening. It is such a stress-releasing hobby that inhibits the inconvenience of going to the gym or elsewhere. It becomes a good avenue of distraction to take our focus off the problems we deal with on a daily basis. It is an activity that requires dedication and work, but we can see almost immediate results after several days. It is like another version of meditation because it takes your mind away from stress and other negative thoughts. What's more, you can see its beauty once flower buds or new leaves start to form.

De-stress Yourself

A lot of people do not do something to address the stress they're dealing with until physical symptoms are observed and are starting to affect their life and overall well-being. It is very important not to leave stress as it is until it makes you sick. You should learn to identify when you are stressed and make sure that you take action to reduce stress to avoid it from piling up.

Numerous actions can be taken to decrease the risk of being affected by stress, and a lot of them only require simple common sense. Once you have a nagging feeling about the stress that you're dealing with, it is very important to express your concerns to your doctor.

Knowing what stresses you out can help minimize the occurrence of such instances in the future. If you can, try to keep a record of situations that caused a great deal of stress so you know how to deal with them in the future. Bear in mind that there is no such thing as stress-free, but what we can do is keep stress to a minimum. A lot of individuals tend not to include relaxation or vacation in their schedules. This is something that is considered very unhealthy and can affect overall well-being because conscious relaxation is essential to proper bodily function and relieves the mind from the effects of stress.

Managing Time

Effective time management is not limited to accomplishing tasks in a timely and systematic manner. It also lifts you from the preoccupation that you need to accomplish a task at hand. A fact that is often denied by most employees is that the aspect of time management ends as soon as you are done with work. As a professional, you have to understand the importance of "time off." A time off is not simply defined as a day that you are not in the office; you should be able to detach yourself completely, and this includes physical and emotional detachment.

Let's go back to the "Yes" and "No" in day-to-day activities. At work, it is better not to over-commit. You should be able to anticipate if the load is becoming overwhelming. It is normal for us to impress someone in the workplace to show how effective we are, but we have to know our limits because if we don't, we might end up messing up the entirety of the tasks given to us. You should allow yourself to have enough space as a "buffer" when the unexpected comes your way, and every aspect of your system is on heightened alert.

There is Fun Out of Life

Sometimes, when we are lost in a series of choices regarding shutting up or speaking up, we overcomplicate and overanalyze things. This clouds our perception about life, and in the end, we miss the fun part of living. You can plan your day-to-day activities and allocate an hour or two for something that provides you pleasure. When you have something to look forward to, even the littlest of things, it allows your mind to cope more even with the least pleasant aspects of life.

Positivity is the Key

When we are agitated by our actions and haunted by our failures, we become grumpy and worse versions of ourselves. We lose the chance to show the world how awesome we are as a person. Sometimes, a day won't be as bad if we will only allow it to have a dash of positivity. Dwelling on failures will never help you. Always reward yourself for the success you've accomplished, even for the smallest accomplishments. The key to a harmonious exchange of ideas is to understand that everyone, including you, has limits and cannot always succeed. We all have our share of failures but bear in mind that you are not the failure. It is better to reflect on what you have achieved and plan ahead on what more you want to achieve. When you assert yourself in a non-threatening and positive way, it helps you combat stress. Learn to accept that the demands placed on you are only considered as a matter of choice.

When an individual is healthy, he or she can cope better with stress. In fact, poor health can be a major cause of stress. You can add some exercise routines to your schedule to help improve muscle control, get more toned, and gain self-esteem. As much as possible, avoid stimulants or excessive consumption of caffeine.

Get Enough ZZzs

I'm sure you are already aware that in order to function properly, our body needs at least six to eight hours of sleep. This is the only chance that our body can repair and condition itself for the activities the next day. If you are the type of person who neglects sleep to accomplish things at work or school, you might end up experiencing agitation and lack of focus because your mind and body did not receive the rest that it needs.

Shut Up – then Speak Up

You might find it contradicting, but when you learn to shut up in situations that call for it, you also have to learn when to speak up about your emotions. Do not cope with problems alone. It can be such a helpful idea to speak with a friend or someone who understands your situation. Speaking about your sentiments loosens and lightens the burden, as well as reduces emotional buildup that often leads to explosive emotional bursts in the future if left "untreated."

Relaxation and Self-Help

There are a lot of methods to help you reduce stress that can be attributed to situations that require you to shut up or speak up. You can learn a lot of self-help techniques that can be very handy in controlling your emotions even to the most stressful day of your life.

Self-Help Techniques

The options for self-help techniques are almost endless. These induce calmness and reduce accumulated stress and tension. It is known that mindfulness is the most powerful type of relaxation. Despite being the most powerful approach, it is also one of the simplest, because this can be done right there and then at the moment you need it, and it promotes a conscious effect that you can look back on in the future. Through such methods as meditation, regrets and worries that get the best of you will simply drift away.

Creative Visualization

Creative visualization can be loosely associated with daydreaming, except that the former is considered as a somewhat conscious visualization. Imagine yourself peacefully lying in a grassland as your face is gently touched by the fresh breeze, or how believing that you are on that dream vacation of yours where you are in a hammock as you watch the sunset while the waves serenely touch the shore. Creative visualization is an effective and immersive stress diversion because it incorporates the experience internally and psychologically. It induces a relaxed state which eventually drains a significant amount of tension and stress.

Progressive Relaxation

Progressive relaxation involves the relaxation of specific parts of the body until the entire body is completely relaxed. The relaxation method is divided into segments depending on what you think is the most stressed part. Progressive relaxation usually takes about thirty minutes to complete and is considered as one of the most effective methods to achieve physical relaxation. It can be done with a distinct combination of pressure application, stretching, and movement to relieve tensed muscles and alleviate pain caused by stress and agitation.

Calming and Quieting

This process aims to form a channel that diverts the mind from stressful ideas and thoughts and focusing on emotions that induce relaxation. You might be doing this subconsciously, but humming, chanting, or even a relaxed series of inhaling and exhaling can be considered as calming and quieting methods. In addition, counting sheep or staring at green plants or soothing images can be perceived as quieting or calming methods.

Breathing Exercises

Sometimes, we just need to breathe. Breathing exercises can be used to help us release tension. Breathing too rapidly induces agitation while breathing at a relaxed phase promotes relaxation. Inhale, and then exhale. Pace your breathing as you distract yourself from the stress and zero in your focus to your breathing. You will be surprised to feel the stress drifting off. Breathing exercises teach us to calm down and encourage the reduction of physical tension.

Recognition of Tension

This approach allows the individual to clench muscle groups intentionally in successive motion, concentrating on the tension and then voluntary relaxing these muscles. This can be done in areas such as the stomach, hands, and shoulders. It is very important to understand that this is only applicable to mild to moderate tension because voluntary tensing and relaxing the muscles of severely tensed muscles can lead to cramps, which can aggravate the situation. Recognition of tension is considered as a very effective alternative process that allows the muscles to be stretched, therefore effectively releasing tension and normalizing the muscles. This method is very effective when you feel the need to stretch but you cannot get out of a current engagement, such as a meeting or a conference call at work. That way, you can successfully alleviate tension without disrupting your work.

Conclusion

You now know the basics and the most common situations that will give you two choices – to speak up or to shut up. You are now more equipped to deal with stress, and you are now aware of how to de-stress and keep up with challenges that you have to deal with on a daily basis. Now comes the hardest part of this guide, and that is to find your own strength in applying what you have learned, which will help you improve as a person. By applying these techniques, you can become a better version of yourself when it comes to making sound decisions. By now, you are wiser about the battles you have to fight and the scenarios in which shutting up is the better choice. I can say that you can do it. Being capable of doing it does not mean it will be easy, as it will take practice. But when the time comes that you already mastered this skill, which requires a clear mind and a quick response, you will have found a new and improved version of yourself.

Win a free

kindle
OASIS

Let us know what you thought of this book to enter the
sweepstake at:

http://booksfor.review/keepshut

Printed by Amazon Italia Logistica S.r.l.
Torrazza Piemonte (TO), Italy

10643408R00023